GEORGE PERRY

Diana
A celebration

WINDWARD

To be the subject of a score of biographies at only 21 is an achievement worthy of the Guinness Book of Records. To have jumped from comfortable upper-class obscurity to a front-page prominence that would be the envy of any pop or film superstar is amazing indeed. But to retain charm, vivacity, humour and naturalness, when batteries of telephoto lenses are ensuring that millions of viewers around the world will be watching every movement, is the test of true star quality. Diana, the Princess of Wales, is a 'natural', someone born with an essence that the camera loves. She has adapted to the hothouse life of royalty as though all along it had been her proper destiny. She has, with her freshness, her bright youthfulness and her clear-eyed vibrant beauty, given the people of Britain something they had always dreamed about, a consort for the heir to the throne who represented the modern, forward-looking generations, who could become a highly-popular queen and mother. Her children will strengthen the line of the British monarchy, preserving its stability in a world locked in a constant cycle of change. Timing has been on Diana's side. Queen Elizabeth II has reigned for more than 30 years, through a period of rapid and often astonishing social upheaval.

That the British monarchy remains intact while elsewhere so many royal houses have disappeared is as much a measure of the Queen's custodianship as of the innate sense of tradition of the British people. Her reforms have been gradual, but they have been there, and in due course it will be seen that she and the Duke of Edinburgh were wise in not forcing the pace harder, or else Prince Charles, too, would have no throne left to inherit.

There is a love-hate relationship between royalty and the media. The one needs the other, but neither would care openly to admit it. But royalty sells newspapers and pushes up television ratings. Royalty, however, needs and depends on the media to foster and maintain its popularity, enabling the monarchy to fulfil its constitutional duty without voices of dissent undermining its purpose. Not every Briton is pro-Royalist, but opposition is tiny and militant republicanism non-existent.

There is still a necessity for the image to be brightened up from time-to-time, and for a shift of focus to the younger members of the family. From birth in 1948 Prince Charles has earnestly trained for a career that he is unlikely to take up until late middle age. His assiduous application to the innumerable pursuits

regarded as a proper grounding for the Prince of Wales and heir to the throne, be they learning Welsh or how to fly a helicopter, gaining a goodish degree at Cambridge, commanding a naval minesweeper, or jumping out of an aircraft (with parachute), has led him to be regarded as a serious, responsible and able figure, much more of a sobersides than his more dashing younger brother, Andrew. To be fair, he is also known for his sense of humour, inspired in part by vintage *Goon Show* recordings, his fondness for polo, and his girl friends. Of the latter there were many, most if not all of outstanding pedigree and beauty, but not necessarily with the attributes people would want in a future queen.

Charles, sensibly aware that he had plenty of time to make up his mind, sowed his oats, enjoyed himself, and then at 33 chose to marry a girl who had not been gossip column fodder, but had been nearby for a long time.

Diana Frances Spencer, the third daughter of Viscount and Viscountess Althorp, was born on the royal estate of Sandringham, Norfolk on July 1, 1961. Park House is a rambling, undistinguished pile of gabled masonry with ivy-covered walls, standing about half-a-mile from Sandringham House, the monarch's country home since Queen

The infant Diana in her pram at Park House, summer 1962

Diana aged four with brother Charles, now Lord Althorp

Victoria, and the birthplace of Charles's grandfather, King George VI. Diana's grandfather, the fourth Lord Fermoy, leased Park House from George V, and after his death in 1955 his widow Ruth became a lady-in-waiting to the Queen Mother. Her daughter Frances had married Lord Althorp, the son and heir of the seventh Earl Spencer, in the previous year. He had served George VI as an equerry and until his marriage had been in the Queen's household. His own mother was a Lady of the Bedchamber to the Queen Mother from 1937.

So there were plenty of links with royalty, and Diana's childhood was spent in proximity to illustrious neighbours.

Her siblings were Sarah, born in 1955, Jane in 1957 and Charles, who is now Lord Althorp, born in 1964. There was another brother, but he died in 1960, shortly after birth.

What Park House had, and Sandringham House did not, was a swimming pool, and the royal children were delighted to take advantage of it. Prince Andrew, who was born in 1960 and Prince Edward, four years younger, were

Above: *Scotland 1974, and Shetland pony, Soufflé, a holiday friend*
Right: *In London, working with children*

among Diana's earliest playmates, and attended each other's birthday parties. But Prince Charles, 12 years Andrew's senior, dwelt on another planet.

There was also a schoolroom at Park House where Diana first began nursery education, under the supervision of the selfsame governess, Gertrude Allen, known as 'Ally', who had taught her mother a generation earlier when she had been in the employ of the Fermoys.

Diana was only six when storm clouds disturbed her childhood happiness. Her parents' marriage disintegrated, and her mother left Park House suddenly. The new man in her life was Peter Shand Kydd, whom she married two years later in 1969. Although attempts were made to lessen the effect of the split, all good intentions went out of the window when a messy, widely-reported custody battle took place with the result that Lord Althorp kept his children.

In 1968 Diana started to attend a day school in Kings Lynn called Silfield, and

3

Diana with her charges from Young England Kindergarten

The days she can walk alone along a street are almost over

two years later, at the age of 9, she was sent as a boarder to a prep school, Riddlesworth Hall, at Diss, also in Norfolk. Already she had a reputation for easy-going warmth and was especially kind to those pupils not blessed with her self-confidence. She was said to be good at games, particularly swimming, but less adventurous in classroom work, which was average. She was permitted with the others to keep a pet, and a guinea pig of hers actually won a prize. Her love of animals became slightly qualified at the age of 10 when she fell from a horse and broke her arm, and the traditional equine enthusiasm of the royal family wanes a little when it reaches her.

Holidays were spent with her mother, who now had a large estate in Argyll where the outdoor pleasures of hiking across peat bogs, boating and swimming were close at hand. The rest of the time she was at Park House, to which her grandmother, Lady Fermoy, had gone to fill the maternal gap in her life.

At the age of 12 Diana moved on to West Heath, an exclusive and expensive girls' boarding school near Sevenoaks,

Kent, which was also selected by several of her Riddlesworth friends. She had no difficulty in passing the entrance examination. Her best subject was history, although generally she was an unexceptional scholar. In games she excelled, and captained the hockey team as well as winning cups for swimming and diving. She was also a good dancer, and at one time had ambitions to enter the ballet, having had lessons from the age of 3. Her height put a stop to that idea, but nevertheless she won the school dancing prize. She was also given a special award for service, a cup that was only presented if there was someone in the school worthy of it. She showed an interest in helping old people and handicapped children, as well as fellow pupils.

Her Sandringham friend, Prince Andrew, was now at Gordonstoun, and to the envy of her schoolmates she wrote and received letters from him.

In 1975 her paternal grandfather died, her father then becoming the eighth Earl Spencer and inheriting the ancient, partially crumbling, ancestral seat, Althorp in Northamptonshire. The mansion dates from 1508, and although

much-altered over the centuries, is one of Britain's larger stately homes, a veritable treasure house of paintings, sculpture, tapestries, china and furniture, even though some items have been sold to help pay for the maintenance of the estate. The public, admitted at £2 a head, also contributes, and although no overt attempt is made to capitalise on the connection with the Princess of Wales, the number of visitors has multiplied since the wedding.

In 1976 Earl Spencer remarried. His new wife, Raine, was the former Lady Dartmouth, a spectacular public figure in her own right who as a former Westminster city councillor had often stirred up headlines in order to expose sloppiness, official inefficiency and threats to old buildings. Her mother is the prolific novelist and sprightly octogenarian, Barbara Cartland. Again Diana's father became involved in a divorce suit, with the deserted Earl Dartmouth alleging, but not proving, adultery.

The Spencer children were at first apprehensive and wary of their stepmother, who clearly was a strong-willed person, with a proven interest in art and architecture. At once she zestfully applied her energies to restoring Althorp's grandeur. The stuff of which the new Countess was made became apparent in 1978 when Earl Spencer suddenly collapsed with a massive brain haemorrhage. Although he was only 55 it seemed that his time had come, and doctors told her to prepare for the worst. Raine refused to accept their verdict, and urged that they try a new drug of which she had heard. Meanwhile she nursed and coaxed her husband back to consciousness, and while the Earl can never be fully fit again, he is, thanks to her relentless determination, able to live a relatively normal life, and could share to the full the joy of Diana's wedding.

In 1977, having left West Heath at 16, Diana's final educational establishment was the Institut Alpin Videmanette, near Gstaad in Switzerland, a finishing school which had domestic science on its curriculum as well as skiing. Although there were many aspects of the good Swiss life that appealed to her, and opportunities to improve spoken French abounded, Diana stayed for only six weeks of the three-month course on which she had enrolled. The ostensible reason for quitting was homesickness, which was acute. Her sister Sarah happened to be enjoying a skiing holiday at Klösters in a party with the Prince of Wales and the Duke of Gloucester, and Diana was given an indication of what it was like for a young woman to be the object of speculation by the media in its constant hunt for the future bride of the heir to the throne. She even compiled a cuttings book of her sister's gossip column stories. It was not, however, anything more than a passing friendship, and Lady Sarah rapidly faded from Charles's company after inadvertently falling foul of the royal rule – never to talk to the Press about a relationship. But it was during this period that the Prince first became aware of Diana as anything other than a child, during a visit to Althorp in late 1977 as Sarah's guest at a shoot. He later recalled Diana as "an amusing, jolly and attractive 16-year-old" but it was to be another two years before the romance was to develop, and initially there was some friction between the sisters.

Diana had no wish to have a London season, regarding it as something of a charade. She had no intention of burying herself at Althorp, and persuaded her father to buy her a flat in London, in Coleherne Court at the Earls Court end of Old Brompton Road. The lease cost £100,000. Diana was landlady to three other girls, Ann Bolton, Virginia Pitman and an old West Heath friend, Carolyn

Diana poses with two of the kindergarten children in September sunshine, 1980

Pride. Diana had no career ambitions to speak of – she did, however, want to do something more than parties, discos, dinners and frequent holidays, either skiing or lazing on the Shand Kydd's Scottish acres. She had always had a great fondness and way with children, and for a while she worked as a part-time nanny for an American couple stationed in London. In the autumn of 1979 she began a three-day weekly job at the Young England Kindergarten in Pimlico, which was run by a pair of former West Heath pupils, Kay Seth-Smith and Victoria Wilson. It was a job she greatly enjoyed. By now she owned her first car, having passed the driving test at her initial attempt, and was settling into the life of a well-heeled young girl-about-town, not entirely idling her life away while she got on with preparing herself for eventual marriage. As part of that training programme she enrolled in a Cordon Bleu cookery course. Her lifestyle was similar to that of many other girls with her social background, who were not interested in pursuing high-powered careers.

It has been said that such was the determination of Diana to catch her Prince that she already had him in her sights, long before he was aware of it, and that marital ambitions had been formed as early as November 1977 when as a 16-year-old she had followed him around the muddy fields of Althorp while he bagged his game. But she was no recluse at Coleherne Court; all the girls in the flat led busy social lives, and a constant stream of smartly-dressed young men in stockbroking, the estate business or the wine trade crossed the threshhold. More than one of them made a pitch for the tall, tanned blonde, Lady Diana. But the discretion of both her flatmates and her male admirers has remained absolute, to their credit.

In August 1979 Diana was a guest at Balmoral, apparently at the invitation of her old Sandringham friend, Andrew. During the course of the visit horrific news came from Ireland. Lord Mountbatten had been murdered by terrorists. It was an event that cast a heavy cloud over the royal family. Mountbatten had been particularly close to Prince Charles, and there can be no doubt that Diana offered a sympathetic presence during a time of private grief.

Further royal family visits followed. Her second sister, Lady Jane, had

Left: *Smith's Lawn, Windsor – bejeanned Diana*
Right: *Prince Charles and fiancee at Balmoral*

Above left: *Lord Snowdon—informal and formal*
Below left: *Buckingham Palace – and the Queen's approval of the engagement*

married Robert Fellowes, assistant private secretary to the Queen in April 1978, with Diana as bridesmaid, and their baby was a magnet for her attention during her visits.

The first outward sign of interest from Charles came in July 1980 when he invited Diana to watch him play polo at Cowdray in Sussex. Shortly afterwards she was a guest on the royal yacht *Britannia* during Cowes week. The next month she was back at Balmoral.

By now Fleet Street was beginning to sense that the long chase for the future queen might be reaching its climax. The most skilled Charles-watchers were dispatched to the banks of the Dee, armed with long camera lenses and powerful binoculars. The Prince, an old hand at the sport of dodging the Press, managed to win on points, and no clear photographs of his then-unrecognised companion resulted.

But back in London the gossip could not be stifled. The word got around that this time 'the real thing' had happened and the new girl was not to be categorised with the others. The keenest sleuths found out where she lived and even ferreted out her telephone number. Cameramen bivouacked outside Cole-herne Court and waved tenners at anyone willing to pass on helpful inform-ation. The kindergarten was besieged,

Right: *First official outing to Goldsmith's Hall*
Below: *Diana, with Princess Grace*

"Kiss me Hardy!" Nicholas Hardy, Cheltenham schoolboy seizes his moment. "You'll never live this down," said she

much to the amusement of the young children. A photographer was even discovered climbing through the lavatory window. Diana's red Metro became a familiar sight on news bulletins, and her fleetness of foot and delicious smile as she hopped out of it caught the public's fancy. While the inevitable official and semi-official denials were being made she was, by necessity, left to cope with Press interest as best she could – any visible assistance from the Palace would have ensured that the game was up. Her inexperience led her to being pictured in a thin skirt against a sunlit background, an old trick in the glamour photographers' books, but the result was so charming and innocent that the nation applauded. Moreover, she was seen to have superb legs – long, well-shaped and slender but not bony. Britain had a new pin-up.

In a way the period of press barrage was a test of her mettle and her ability to cope with the ordeal was carefully

monitored at the Palace. Charles never once visited her at the flat, and for the most part the courtship was conducted in secret retreats. Eventually Press speculation went too far, and the *Sunday Mirror* printed a story that Lady Diana and the Prince had spent the night together on the royal train while it was parked in a siding during one of his official visits. The denials from the Palace were indignant and an apology was demanded, but not made.

The constant pursuit of Diana made her life almost intolerable, preventing her from going anywhere without photographers following her. No longer could she trust that innocent remarks made to people she did not know very well would not end up in a gossip column. On more than one occasion she burst into tears as the chase became too hot. Her mother, Mrs Peter Shand Kydd, wrote to *The Times*, pleading for Fleet Street to leave her daughter alone. Even the Queen, normally placid and reticent,

became waspish when the lensmen hoved into sight, and Charles was moved to wish their editors "a particularly nasty New Year."

In the early autumn he had bought a house in the country, a Georgian mansion just a mile from Tetbury, Gloucestershire, and only six miles from Gatcombe Park, the home of Princess Anne and Captain Mark Phillips. Highgrove House had even been on their shopping list when they were house-hunting, but was rejected on account of the proximity of the nearby main road. Charles had invited Diana to his house, and she had offered several suggestions as to how it should be decorated before the work was handed over to a professional, Dudley Poplak.

In the New Year the Prince spent a skiing holiday at Klösters without Diana, while she prepared to escape from all the attention she had been getting by going to Australia, and staying on her mother's sheep station. At the beginning of Feb-

May 1981. Diana in Tetbury, soon to be her new hometown

A resounding, joyful welcome from Gloucestershire people

ruary, Prince Charles, after a dinner in his rooms at Buckingham Palace, finally made his proposal to her. "I thought it would be a good idea," he said in his engagement interview, "that apart from anything else, if she went to Australia she could then think about it." It seems that his precautions were not needed – her reaction, in spite of the change it would make to her life, was a rapid acceptance.

An unexpected tragedy occurred just before the engagement, with Diana as an onlooker. Charles's favourite steeple-chaser, Allibar, died from a heart attack under him while being exercised at Lambourn. The Prince was greatly upset by the loss.

Diana's flatmates, whose loyalty could be counted upon, were told that the engagement had taken place, but the public announcement had still to be made. Charles, with an old-fashioned notion of doing the right thing, sought out Diana's father, and addressing him

as 'sir' requested his daughter's hand in marriage. The startled Earl afterwards playfully speculated on what would have happened if he had said "No!" Nothing, however, would have caused him to obstruct her happiness, and he was proud to give his blessing.

Diana's Australian holiday, even though much of it was spent in the remote sheep-grazing Murrumbidgee area of New South Wales, proved to be no respite from reporters, and the antipodean kind were more intrepid than those at home. Peter Shand Kydd's staff mounted a shotgun watch on the sheep station, and even Prince Charles had difficulty making telephone contact.

But absence consolidated her feelings, as well as giving her the chance to seek her mother's approval.

On Tuesday, February 24, 1981 the announcement of the engagement was made by Buckingham Palace. Crowds gathered around the Victoria Memorial, while in the forecourt the band of the

Coldstream Guards repeatedly played the banal sometime Eurovision songhit "Congratulations."

The ring was a huge sapphire set within a gold circlet with 14 diamonds, and was alleged to have cost the Prince £30,000 from Garrards. A photocall took place on the garden front of the Palace, and for the first time, in spite of all their pre-engagement efforts, Fleet Street got pictures of the couple together. It did not go unnoticed that Charles stood on a step behind his fiancee to make a satisfactory composition and to counter her splendid height. At Coleherne Court a permanent police guard shooed off loiterers. Diana was now 'official' and entitled to a new set of privileges.

Even Earl Spencer and the Countess were among the joyful crowds. He told reporters that even as a baby she had been a "superb physical specimen".

The Prince of Wales, facing the Press, said "I'm amazed she's been brave enough to take me on." He became

Getting used to hat-wearing – at Nicholas Soames' wedding

Right: *Diana, the Queen Mother, Princess Margaret and best man, Prince Charles as his friend Nicholas Soames gets married*

understandably nervous when someone asked him if they were in love. He answered affirmatively, adding "whatever 'in love' means".

Diana now gave up her kindergarten job, moved out of her flat, and went to Clarence House for the first stage in what was to be a crash course in how to be royal. The engagement period was to last for five months, with the wedding taking place on July 29, not at Westminster Abbey, the traditional venue for such events, but at St Paul's Cathedral. It was their personal choice – the cathedral had room for a larger congregation, the acoustics were better capable of satisfying their mutual love of music, and the processional route was doubled in length, offering enhanced opportunities

for the crowds to catch sight of them on the great day.

The nation became gripped in an epidemic of Di-fever. Shopgirls and typists quickly began to copy her look, with the famous fringe hairstyle and its artful highlights, the dark eye make-up, the young style dresses, the knickerbockers, the dungarees, the low-heeled shoes, the Laura Ashley prints. Newspapers vied with each other in producing punning headlines with 'Di' in them. The worst was probably 'See Nipples and Di' after her first public engagement with her fiance, at a gala evening in aid of the Royal Opera House, held at Goldsmiths' Hall. She wore a stunning black strapless taffeta dress, held up by minimal boning and

willpower. It was a brilliant creation of David and Elizabeth Emanuel, and its impact eclipsed even the eternal effervescence of Princess Grace of Monaco. Once again Fleet Street leapt tactlessly in with both feet, and a popular paper tried to allege that a shadow across her breast was more than normally meets the eye. An action replay was solemnly conducted on News at Ten and proved it was pure illusion.

The Emanuels were awarded the coveted honour of fashioning the wedding dress, in spite of the criticism of Prudence Glynn, alias Lady Windlesham, for many years *The Times* fashion editor, who declared in the *International Herald Tribune* that Lady Diana was a fashion disaster. Certainly her tastes

were refreshingly different from those normally prevailing in the royal family. Extremes of any form have been frowned upon ever since the former Prince of Wales, later the Duke of Windsor, affected loud checks and a singularly sloppy way of doing up his necktie. Charles's own clothes are so unremarkable as to be unnoticed, and the conservative cut of his suits enables them to soldier on for years without anyone being the wiser.

Part of Diana's fashion indoctrination at Palace insistence was the need to wear a hat, an ageing accessory for a girl of 19. Tentatively at first, but with increasing confidence, Diana sported colourful headgear, usually from the hand of John Boyd, and eventually turned a dull convention into a personal triumph.

In March Prince Charles embarked on a strenuous five-week tour which was to take him to Australia, New Zealand and Canada. There had been a certain amount of discussion on the possibility of his appointment as Australia's governor-general, his brief attendance at Geelong having thought to have been an advantage. The political climate, however, did not favour such a proposition, and it was quietly dropped. The engaged couple had a tearful parting at the airport, and during the course of the tour Charles was noticeably less buoyant than usual, a condition

Above: *Trooping of the Colour 1981. The flypast*
Left: *At visit of late King Khalid of Saudi Arabia*
Below: *Riding to the Trooping with Andrew*

tactlessly made worse by the abundance of media-crazy Diana replicas who thrust themselves at him at various stages of the journey. There was also the awkward matter of the alleged royal tapes, supposedly the result of someone tapping the telephone during the Prince's strained long-distance conversations with his betrothed. The fuss abated when the published version was palpably exposed as a crude hoax.

On his way back to Britain, Charles came via Washington, where he called

on President Reagan who made the pardonable gaffe of accepting an invitation to the wedding even before one had been issued. (In the event he didn't make it, Nancy, the First Lady, standing in instead.) On arrival back at RAF Lossiemouth Charles wasted no time and hastened to Balmoral for a happy reunion with Diana, who had flown to Scotland through a raging thunderstorm in order to be with him. They were then able to take a few days off, and obliged the inevitable photographers with a rustic photocall on a corner of the estate.

The pressures on Diana increased even more during the run-up period to the day itself. She was given many chances to become used to the demands made to royalty – the walkabouts, the waving to the crowds, the shaking of hundreds of hands until the fingers began to feel paralysed, the need to be seen smiling at all times in public no matter what the feet were saying privately. There was just one occasion when the pace became too much for her, and at a polo match in which the Prince was playing the cameras caught her rushing from the field in tears, with an anxious Charles later consoling her.

Meanwhile, her portrait, painted by Bryan Organ, was unveiled in the National Portrait Gallery with due ceremony. She watched John McEnroe

Above: *Lady Diana sparkling in a sea of grey toppers at Ascot*

Left: *Her Ascot outfit worn with pearl choker*

beat Bjorn Borg at Wimbledon and went to Royal Ascot. She flitted back and forth from the Emanuels and their Brook Street premises, where the wedding dress was being made in conditions of great secrecy. The mood of the nation was subtly being brought to a head for the wedding eve, which she spent in the security of Clarence House while a massive firework display took place in Hyde Park, attended by large numbers of distinguished wedding guests, some of them crowned, who made their journey in a fleet of specially-chartered coaches normally used for tourist sightseeing.

It was unfortunate that the pleasant pyrotechnics of the celebrations were countered by an explosion of street rioting in Toxteth, a symptom of the discontent that simmered a little beneath

the surface in a Britain where three million people were now unemployed. In some quarters the panoply and stage management in which obscure courtiers with improbable titles suddenly assumed important functions was seen as a huge smokescreen to mask the problems and suffering that existed in the country. Ken Livingstone, the controversial newly-elected leader of the Greater London Council, had publicly declined his official invitation to St Paul's and said that he would be at his desk as usual on July 29, which had been proclaimed a national holiday.

In spite of such occasional killjoys, it was a tremendous day. The Mall was a dense mass of people who had in some cases crossed oceans just to be there. The American TV networks transferred entire programme teams to the British capital, and for a week the rival breakfast shows, NBC's *Today* and ABC's *Good*

Morning America were transmitted live from London, leaving no cliché unturned from the scores of royal pundits enlisted to 'interpret' the goings-on for viewers in the United States. The happy couple had given a relaxed interview of their own to the BBC and ITV for the wedding eve. Although the questions of Angela Rippon and Andrew Gardner were phrased respectfully and clearly carefully vetted in advance, some of the responses had a touch of informality. Asked if the Prince had been a help to her in the preceding months, Diana averred that he had been marvellous, a tower of strength, and then noticing his pleased expression, added: "I had to say that because you're sitting there!"

The eyes of the world on wedding morning were focussed on the narrow carriageway connecting Clarence House to the Mall as the bride's coach appeared in the warm July sunshine. She could not

fail to look radiant, dressed by the Emanuels, made up by Barbara Daly, coiffed by her favourite hairdresser, Kevin Shanley. The dress was shaped out of 44 yards of ivory-coloured silk – a crinoline worn over layers of net. The enormous sleeves were edges with lace. Any fears that the Emanuels would repeat the plunging décolletage of the Goldsmiths' Hall gala were immediately allayed – the neckline was a discreetly-masked 'V'. The train was 25 feet long, but the bride entered the great Cathedral without a falter, on the arm of her father, who, no longer a fit man, required her help to make it up the aisle.

It was the first royal wedding to be conducted by Dr Robert Runcie, the Archbishop of Canterbury. He spoke of the fairy tale element that formed the people's view of the Charles and Diana story, but went on to tell the royal pair that this was the point where the adventure really began – that all couples on their wedding day were 'royal couples' charged with creating each other and a more loving world.

It was a satisfying spectacle. The choral singing and the magnificent voice of Kiri Te Kanawa gave public notice of Charles and Diana's fondness of music. Not an inch of space was to spare inside the cathedral, but television viewers were probably able to see more of the ceremony than many present, and to hear the occasional fumbled line, such as when Diana got her new husband's Christian names in the wrong order, and he forgot to preface 'goods' with 'worldy'. The *sotto voce* "Well done!" whispered by the Prince when Diana had said her vows was clearly heard. It was to the most stirring of Elgar's works, *Pomp and Circumstance No 1*, that they left as man and wife, and faced outside the ringing cheers of the crowds gathered atop Ludgate Hill. The return procession gave a generous eyeful to onlookers, with the objects of their attention riding in an open landau. The crowds outside the Palace received a further delight

Two days later they were on their way again, this time to Eastleigh Airport and a ponderously slow flight to Gibraltar in an Andover of the Queen's Flight. The choice of Gibraltar for the commencement of the main part of the honeymoon, which was to be spent on the royal yacht *Britannia*, had sparked off a diplomatic row preventing the King and Queen of Spain from attending the wedding. It had been regarded as tactless to involve a territory whose sovereignty was disputed by its close neighbour. Perhaps it was fortunate that the direction in which *Britannia* was to sail was eastward into the Mediterranean, not south towards the Falklands. It was to the Greek islands that they went, in the company of a

Above and left: *Days at the races. Diana goes to Royal Ascot, June 1981*
Right: *The Prince takes to the polo field at Windsor*

when during the balcony appearance the couple exchanged, on Diana's instigation, a warm and perfectly-connected kiss. Even the wedding group photographs by Lord Lichfield had an unprecedented informality, exactly expressing the happiness of the day.

The going-away outfit was a coral pink Bellville Sassoon suit, worn with a pearl choker and a jaunty, feathered Robin Hood-style hat. Behind the landau bobbed a number of plastic balloons with the Prince's insignia on them, and a crudely-scrawled 'Just Married' sign hung below. The coach made its way to Waterloo where a special train at a red-carpeted Platform 12 whisked them to Romsey, Hampshire, and the first two days of their honeymoon at Broadlands, the home of Lord Mountbatten, where the Queen and Prince Philip had spent part of their honeymoon in 1947.

ship's crew of 270, trained to carry out orders from silent signals.

A short visit was made at Port Said on the President of Egypt, Anwar Sadat, who entertained them to a sumptuous banquet. A matter of weeks later he was assassinated in horrifyingly cold-blooded circumstances.

From Egypt they flew directly to Scotland for the last phase of the honeymoon, spent at Balmoral. Pedants of royal matters noted that north of the border Diana was not 'Princess of Wales' but 'Duchess of Rothesay', although it is unlikely that anyone would be confused.

It was now that Britain slowly came off the euphoric high it had been on throughout the summer. The Princess attended the Braemar Gathering (a much larger turnout than usual was noted) wearing the snazziest of Caroline Charles outfits, and looked as Scottish as a chorus girl in *Brigadoon*, but such is the strength of her personality and style there were no objectors.

In London, however, her portrait by Bryan Organ in the NPG was defaced by a vandal. Crowds lined up for hours to see the display of wedding presents, valued at £5 million, at St James's Palace, and Diana, on a short break, went to see them for herself. The newspapers compensated for lack of good stories coming from Scotland with a brouhaha over stag-shooting – it was said that the Princess, whose love of animals was well-publicised, had succumbed to the royal penchant for slaughtering the large, inoffensive beasts that roamed the Highlands, and that she had wounded a deer, leaving it to limp away to an untidy death. Naturally there were denials.

Eventually the long honeymoon ended, almost with a sense of relief that life could now be tackled in earnest. The royal family's customary long summer sojourn at Balmoral is deliberately undertaken to charge up the batteries for the exhausting series of duties that fill the schedules from the autumn.

Diana's induction into the busy round was planned to be relatively gentle, with the Prince carrying the full brunt. No man in Britain more than he has been trained in the delicate task of meeting and making small talk with boring local dignitaries, expressing interest in the most arcane of manufacturing processes shown him by nervous overseers, listening to speeches of mind-stultifying tedium and munching his way through monotonous, semi-digestible meals in the company of unctuous worthies, jockeying among themselves for his

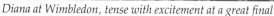

Diana at Wimbledon, tense with excitement at a great final

She joins the standing ovation for the new tennis champion

attention. For them it is the moment of a lifetime. For the Prince there is another town hall to visit tomorrow, another factory line to inspect, another shopping centre in which to go 'walkabout'. That any man could stay sane given such a life is remarkable. That Prince Charles presents an unflagging interest and patience, never for a moment allowing others to become uncomfortable, is a measure of the calm professionalism he brings to his job. It is not an easy skill, but its mastery has evoked admiration for the British monarchy throughout the world, with the Queen setting the finest example. For Diana it was a hard act to follow. Unlike her new in-laws she had, although closely-connected to those in court circles, not been born to fulfil the role. But then, neither had the Queen

Mother, who as Elizabeth Bowes-Lyon had married Charles's grandfather, King George VI when he was Duke of York, and not expected to inherit the throne.

For that reason the Queen Mother was an excellent mentor, and from her Diana learned many of the secrets of how to deal with the stresses of a royal visit, how to wave and smile and simply keep going without faltering, and how to ensure that her own unique personality would surface and survive.

The latter was to be Diana's special asset. Throughout the pre-wedding ordeal she had demonstrated to the world that she could not only stand up to the onslaught of attention, but cope with it in a charming, idiosyncratic way. She had shouldered the immensely awesome task of becoming the wife of

the heir to the throne, without letting her individuality be squashed. There were fears that the machine of monarchy would swallow up and transmogrify her. So far there have been no signs of that happening, and while the Princess of Wales will have forfeited the freedom to walk by herself down a London street window-shopping, to hail a taxi, to drop in on friends unannounced, to grab a meal in a snackbar, to wander round a supermarket, to do a thousand things that the rest of the population take absolutely for granted, she is still clearly of the human race. In fact, she has had a corresponding effect on the Court, the badly-needed breath of fresh air blowing

Right: *A night at the movies – at premiere of For Your Eyes Only at the Odeon Leicester Square*

The new Princess of Wales at Broadlands, the Hampshire home of Lord Mountbatten, two months before her wedding, when an exhibition was opened honouring his memory

Fellowes, Diana's sister, and her husband, live in the Old Barracks.

The three-floor apartment has to provide accommodation for the Prince's staff, which is kept busy, not only keeping his engagements straight and administering the multifarious posts he holds in a large number of organisations, but watching over the extensive interests of the Duchy of Cornwall. Charles, as the Duke, is one of Britain's most powerful landlords, and such is the extent of the annual income from the estates that he does not draw any money from the Civil List. With a new wife to look after it was necessary for him to award himself a 50 per cent pay rise, bringing his salary from the Duchy to £375,000 a year, a sum on which even a prince should be able to support his princess. The gesture did not go unobserved in a country where most workers were held to a pay rise norm in single figures.

Space also had to be provided for the ladies-in-waiting, as well as staff quarters. And naturally a nursery, with playroom and nanny's room adjoining. As at Highgrove, Dudley Poplak was given the decorating job.

Charles said of marriage: "A woman not only marries a man – she marries into a way of life, a job." There was to be no question, from the outset, that Lady Diana would not be at his side for many of his engagements. It was clearly something that was expected of him by the public, and on occasions since his engagement there were frissons of disappointment when he turned up at events in a solo capacity, or he would be jokily asked by wags in the crowd: "How's the missus?"

The Princess was also to cultivate special interests of her own, and to take on some functions independently of the Prince. She would have to face the prospect of one or more gruelling overseas tours for the rest of her life, with pregnancy the only acceptable excuse for ducking out of them.

Her wardrobe would be one of her most time-consuming pre-occupations. There has to be an appropriate garment for every occasion. Diana's dress sense was, before her marriage, on a par with most girls of her class living the life of the 'Sloane Ranger'. Sleek Knightsbridge boutiques could meet most of her needs. She likes informality, and had an abundant collection of various jeans, designer-labelled or otherwise. She wore

Right: Diana always finds time to talk to the children. Broadlands May 1981

down the stuffy Palace corridors. Royal popularity has soared with the advent of Diana, bringing, as *The Times* put it, a touch of romance in a grey world.

The London home for the newlyweds was to be part of Kensington Palace, the redbrick Wren building overlooking the west side of Kensington Gardens and the Round Pond by which many a nanny from a famous family has sat resting her feet, conferring with her sisters while her charge sailed a model boat. Until his marriage Charles had lived at Buckingham Palace, but now an apartment in the

north-west wing of the palace in which Queen Victoria was born was made available to him, after much refurbishment. During the Second World War Kensington Palace was bombed, and it had taken more than 30 years for full-scale restoration.

It is a discreet enclave of royalty. Princess Margaret lives there, as do Prince and Princess Michael of Kent, and the Duke and Duchess of Gloucester. There is also a small pied-à-terre occasionally used by Princess Alexandra and Angus Ogilvy. And Lady Jane

Left: *Aboard the royal yacht Britannia for a cruise to the Greek Islands, and then on to Egypt for a greeting from President Sadat.*
Above: *Homecoming – the suntanned couple arrive back from Egypt. The Princess wore the same coat when she set out*
Right *She takes memories of the Mediterranean to Balmoral*

dungarees to Cowdray Park with the aplomb of an accomplished head-turner. The famous blue Cojano silk suit in the engagement pictures was bought off-the-peg at Harrods the day before. Her honeymoon outfit at Balmoral where she appeared with a kilted Charles for the benefit of photographers consisted of a hound's tooth check blouse and skirt by Bill Pashley. At the Braemar Gathering she drew gasps of admiration from the husky Scots in her Caroline Charles tartan ensemble, topped with a black tam-o'-shanter.

Her favourite designers would appear to be Bellville and Sassoon, Jasper Conran, Donald Campbell and the Emanuels – an eclectic British group. Both her sisters had briefly worked as fashion assistants at *Vogue*, but Diana

Above and right: *At the Braemar Gathering – the Prince superbly kilted, the Princess's tartan by Caroline Charles*
Left: *Balmoral photocall. Pressmen gave her a bouquet – "You'll put it on expenses, I suppose!" quipped Diana*

lacked such a brief, helpful grounding, and was later given some pointers by staff of the magazine. She has made mistakes, sometimes over-compensating to a ludicrous degree, and at her age she may well be sensitive, if not downright embarrassed by criticism. Some advice, however well-meaning, can have a negative effect, and the best is an encouragement to trust her instincts to achieve the most satisfactory results, eschewing the fussy hats, gloves and handbags considered *de rigueur* for royals.

As a perceptive fashion commentator, Meriel McCooey of *The Sunday Times*, put it: "She's incredibly pretty – she looks wonderful in casuals, and fantastic in full evening fig. But she can be mediocre in the middle."

Clearly the lessons are being learned, and it is hoped that as she grows older she will not lose the panache and sparkle her appearances invariably generate. Her height has made flat shoes fashionable, and if she is in the Prince's company she must take care that she does not appear to tower over him, which would be possible in high heels.

For the first of her public duties at the end of the honeymoon a trip to Wales was ordained. It was a significant gesture – the Welsh were anxious to see their new Princess ahead of the rest of Great Britain and would have been hurt had they been denied that privilege. It was really a royal mini-tour, lasting a mere three days and covering 400 miles. The first found them in Caernarvon, where

the Prince had taken his vows in the Investiture of 1969. Greeting them at the Castle was Lord Snowdon, whose brilliant engagement portraits had done much to promote the couple's joyful aspect, but now his cameras were tucked away as he was acting in his official role as Constable of Caernarvon Castle. The royal couple sat on the slate seats in the same spot occupied by the Prince alone 12 years earlier, and listened to the singing of Welsh children.

The Princess's choice of dress was particularly fortunate, an outfit from Donald Campbell in the Welsh national colours of red and dark green. It was the stuff to raise the cheers.

Inevitably a handful of Welsh nationalists tried to put a damper on things, but their denunciatory placards urging the 'English princess' to go home were barely noticed. It was, in any case, another test of Diana's mettle. She acquitted herself nobly. The tour was by most standards of royal progresses minor, but as a first time out for Diana it must have been very strenuous. She gathered flowers by the armful as she made her walkabouts, and began to learn the art of deftly off-loading informally-presented bouquets after a suitable interval. In Cardiff she delighted the City Council by accepting the Freedom of the City in Welsh.

Her naturalness and captivating charm stirred the Welsh into a sudden and almost possessive pride in their new Princess. Children and old-age pensioners were equally entranced. Charles was reduced, as he later put it, to "a mere collector of flowers."

It was noticed that one of the places during her tour of the Principality that received special attention was the maternity wing of a hospital at Pontypool, and she was seen to discuss the problems of labour with a number of the new mothers she met, inevitably sparking off more speculation.

There was abundant evidence of her love of children. She made a point of talking to them whenever she could as she walked past the crowds eager to see her. Even when an insistent Welsh drizzle made the second day of the tour difficult she still strolled among the people clad in a beige raincoat. What particularly touched the onlookers was her spontaneous response to unforeseen moments and her smile, which she

Left: *Royal tour of Wales: the Princess at Caernarvon Castle*
Right: *The dazzling beauty of the new Princess*

maintained without a hint of it being forced. Even her small talk had a refreshing quality, and she projected genuine warmth. She greeted the people as much as they welcomed her, and was heard to exclaim "Thank you" as she waved. The crowds loved the way she would plant kisses, not only on those she knew, such as Lord Snowdon, but also on unfamiliar and delighted infants.

The tour was an overwhelming success in spite of the occasional stinkbombs and flour hurled at the car, and a delightful initiation for the newest member of the royal family.

She was next on view in London, attending the opening of the London Film Festival with Prince Charles. Diana wore an attractive black velvet dress with a high collar for the occasion.

Two days later she attended for the first time a great annual State event, the formal opening by the Sovereign of Parliament. It is a big show, with horse-drawn carriages, full dress uniforms, state trumpeters and tiaras. Diana and Charles rode to Westminster in the coach which had borne her to St Paul's a few months earlier, this time in the company of Princess Anne and Captain Phillips. During the Queen's speech, traditionally the Government's programme of legislation for the coming year, she sat with her husband to the left of the throne, facing an assembly of peers in robes and full-bottomed wigs. She wore a Bellville Sassoon white dress in chiffon, with a dazzling tiara.

The same evening she went to the Victoria and Albert Museum, where a gala was taking place to celebrate the opening of *The Splendours of the Gonzaga*, an exhibition of Renaissance. Another astonishing off-the-shoulder dress was worn, with a delicate ruffled cape shimmering with sequins, and a six-stranded pearl choker, a jewellery item she is fond of, having worn one with her going-away outfit. Perched on a red velvet chair during the speeches she showed occasional signs of weariness – it had, after all, been an arduous week.

The next day the Palace made an announcement. 'The Princess of Wales is expecting a baby next June.' It was then learned that the real reason for her trips from Balmoral to London during the

A Princess of Wales in Wales
Left: *Swansea gala night*
Above: *The famous constant smile*
Far right: *Visit to a maternity wing at the Llwynpia Hospital in the Rhondda*
Below: *Smiling in the rain, unaffected by the Welsh weather*

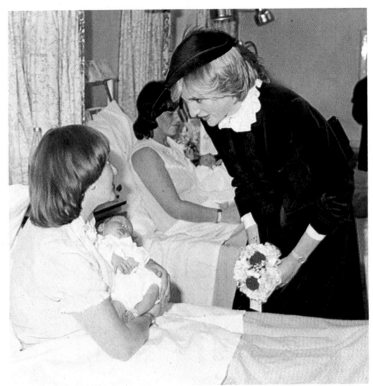

On her way to a gala evening of Welsh music and dance in Swansea, she catches the camera flashes

latter part of the honeymoon was to visit the Queen's gynaecologist, George Pinker. The brevity and directness of the announcement were in keeping with the trend towards unstuffiness set by her. In the past such announcements were not made until about the fourth month of pregnancy, and until recent years merely said that no further engagements would be undertaken, leaving the nation to draw its own conclusions. Now Britain was receiving the news within days of it becoming known inside the family.

There was a trip planned to take her to Australia and New Zealand in 1982 which had to be deferred. It was in New Zealand only two weeks earlier that the Queen had been told by Graham Latimer, president of the Maori Council, at a country festival, that there were rumours she was soon to be a grandmother again. "If it's not true," he said in his speech with a forthrightness not shared by his United Kingdom counterparts, "then the message I have for you is to tell Prince Charles to get on with the job!"

The Queen and Prince Philip, knowing of the jocularity prevailing in parts of the Commonwealth, were not offended but laughed heartily.

It is customary for children to appear fairly quickly in royal marriages. Charles himself was born on November 14, 1948, just inside a year from his parents' wedding on the preceding November 20. The protection of the line is an important consideration, and a long period of childlessness creates some unease. But in any case, given Diana's fondness for children it was unlikely that she would have delayed starting a family. She has made it very clear that more will follow. Both Charles and Diana have three siblings apiece, and are accustomed to the idea of large families.

The first child, Prince William, has immediately become second-in-line to the throne after his father, so the new baby is of very great importance indeed.

The Princess's first public appearance following the announcement was the same day at the Guildhall where she and the Prince were lunching. The Lord Mayor of London dipped into his bag of metaphors and observed that babies were "bits of stardust blown from the hand of God." Diana blushed, and Charles, a proud father-to-be, beamed.

There was a new flurry of headlines. Suddenly all eyes were on Diana's

Prince and Princess at London's National Film Theatre, for the opening night of the 25th London Film Festival, and to see the Australian Film, Gallipoli

waistline, seeking the minutest sign of expansion, even though there were still seven months to go. A deluge of messages of congratulation descended on Highgrove, each one to be properly acknowledged. The Gloucestershire locals had another excuse to imbibe strong spirits in their excellent pubs.

But clearly one era had ended. The lithe, lively Lady Di had gone, now replaced by a burgeoning expectant mother. It was a new persona for the country to get to know, a fresh role for their favourite princess. Anxious articles discussed the incidence of her morning sickness, and the incipient strains of bearing a child who could eventually inherit the throne. Pregnancy can have

Above left: *Riding to the State Opening of Parliament in her wedding coach.*
Left: *Seated with the heir to the throne during the traditional ceremony in House of Lords.*
Above: *That same evening, at the Victoria and Albert Museum for gala opening of The Splendours of the Gonzaga exhibition*

its special traumas and although it was indicated that as many of the engagements in the programme as possible would be carried out, inevitably there were cancellations.

There were many who regretted that she had not had the chance to enjoy her

new status for a while untrammelled by the responsibilities of motherhood. It had been hoped in some quarters that she and the Prince could have become a glamorous jet-setting duo, igniting fashionable places with their magical presence. The emergence into the spotlight for Diana had been very brief – in just a year she had burst into the headlines as the likely bride for Charles, and here within a few weeks of the end of the fairytale honeymoon it was over. Somehow, no one ever thinks of Snow White becoming pregnant.

At an early stage it was announced that Charles intended to follow the advice of Mr Pinker and be present when his wife gave birth, and he did.

"No one told me I was going to feel like this," said the Princess to a sympathetic observer during one of her 'normal' engagements. A trip to the Duchy of Cornwall lands had to be cancelled, much to the disappointment of the ducal tenants anxious to touch forelocks to their new mistress.

In a fine November drizzle she carried out her first solo performance, the switching-on of the Christmas lights in Regent Street. She made a short, but effective speech from a balcony while agitated officials hoisted umbrellas to shield the rain from her midnight blue velvet suit. It had been a long time since the festive illuminations in the West End's major shopping street had attracted so much publicity. Charles, she said, was home watching television.

Two days later she was off on her own again, this time to open a new head Post Office in Northampton, the county town of the shire in which Althorp is located. It provided her with an opportunity to lunch with her father and stepmother. Earl Spencer had been heard to say ruefully that he wasn't seeing much of his daughter since her elevation.

The unwholesome discovery was made by Prince Charles that had already been spotted by his sister. Highgrove was too visible from the main road. Traffic coming out of Tetbury has a clear view of the house, and the only hostelry in the town with accommodation was soon permanently booked with journalists. Cameras with 500 mm lenses were trained on the house and its occupants, while the Princess's short foray into the small town to visit a sweetshop, no doubt to satisfy a pregnancy craving, was shadowed with vigour by the Press, and her modest purchases of chocolates and chewy sweets solemnly listed the next day. It was not merely Fleet Street that displayed such an avid interest in the most mundane of the Princess's activities. Tetbury had overnight become a centre for the international press corps, with contingents of cameramen from

Right: *A beautiful dress for the V & A reception*
Below: *With London's Lord Mayor after Palace announcement of the forthcoming baby*

Above: *The eve before the baby announcement*
Right: *Lunch at the Guildhall the next day*

Europe, the United States and even Japan, sleuthing for pictures. Overseas, photographs were published that went beyond British taste, and faked pasteup work in one Latin-American country even implied that the Princess had posed for a brassiere advertisement.

Enough was enough. The Queen took the unprecedented step of summoning the editors of Fleet Street to the Palace. There her Press Secretary told them that the attention the Princess was getting was a cause of great concern, as much for her health as her dignity.

The Queen discussed the problem with them over drinks – the informality of the approach in itself demonstrating the easing of Palace protocol. The Queen, far from being apprehensive or dismayed by Diana's impact in the preceding months, revealed herself as a proud mother-in-law anxious to protect her from further unfair pummelling.

It would be hard enough for anyone born to it, the Queen told them, but for Diana a sacrifice of fundamental privacy was too much to expect. Public occasions were one thing, but off-duty it was another. She asked that the British Press at least should back off and leave the Princess alone. It was during this meeting that the then editor of *The News of the World* suggested that if the Princess was so desperate for a packet of winegums she should send a footman out for them. The Queen sharply retorted that this was one of the most

pompous remarks that she had ever heard (a well-known ploy used by her to deflate those with whom she is not in accord, apparently), but it was entirely coincidental that her victim was soon afterwards toppled from his post.

The immediate effect of the appeal was a lessening of activity. But there was another side to the story. Out there was a public thirsting for Di news. Newspapers are obliged to sell in order to stay in business. Those which fail to satisfy their readers are replaced by those which do. Tough commercial decisions are made in news selection – it does not, contrary to ill-informed opinion, just

happen. The British royal family has always been a news source, and some papers maintain entire departments to gather it. Nor is such interest confined only to the lower end of the spectrum. *The Times* is one of the most authoritative chronicles of royal events, and its Court Circular an essential diary.

The operation of the monarchy is a curious combination of a highly-visible public display which involves the Queen and other members of the family in a myriad of observable functions at levels ranging from glittering State occasions such as the welcoming of heads of state from other countries, Trooping the

Above left: *Cheers at Chesterfield – the Town Hall*
Below left: *A day at York and Chesterfield.*
Above: *Solo engagement – Regent Street lights*

Colour, the State Opening of Parliament, to such low-key events as opening a new ward in a small country hospital. The other part is the unpublicised but constant reference to the affairs of the nation. The Queen normally has a weekly audience with her prime minister, and daily receives boxes of papers from Whitehall. A parliamentary bill does not become an act until it receives the royal assent. But she is above politics and does not intercede in the democratic processes of government. The crown is the constant bulwark on which the British constitutional structure rests, and the monarch is the barrier against violent change. In the 30-year reign of Elizabeth II she has had eight prime ministers. Thus her knowledge of politics is unique.

But the monarchy also occupies a mystical place in the British national character. Other countries have found it perfectly possible to combine democracy with republicanism. Anti-royalists would argue that the monarchic system is expensive, anachronistic and unnecessary. Nevertheless, other nations look with fascination and even envy at the British, who have shown that monarchy actually works. America, the leading democracy in the world, contains some of the Queen's most fervent admirers.

It is to bolster the mysticism that so much newspaper ink, so many magazine pages are devoted to publicising the royal family. It has to be remembered that much of what they do does not get into headlines, but only makes the local press. But it provides an enriching element in the social formulation of Britain. Already the Princess of Wales is patron of three children's charities: the Albany Community Centre in south-east London, the Malcolm Sargent Cancer Fund for Children and the Pre-school Playgroups Association. She is also the patron of the Royal School for the Blind, and the Welsh National Opera. Many more are likely to follow as her interests develop and broaden. But each member of the royal family has a raftfull of such honorary offices. The organisations concerned benefit from their patronage, and are seen to be on the map. It counts, however subtly, to have royal acknowledgement. If the royal in question is a more attractive member of the clan the benefit appreciates accordingly.

The price that royalty pay is a constant public interest in them. They are used to being stared at, and have a repertory of methods to deal with awkward situations.

None was potentially harder than the evening in which Princess Anne was confronted by an armed gunman in the Mall. During the Balmoral part of the honeymoon Prince Charles had to go to Egypt for the state funeral of President Anwar Sadat, assassinated by plotters at a military display. Only a few weeks earlier he and Diana had dined at his table. The tragedy was a reminder of the dangers high position can hold. Royal security in Britain is handled discreetly, but nevertheless is there to face the most drastic emergency. Diana's own personal detective, a member of the Metropolitan Police, is Graham Smith, who used to be assigned to Princess Anne. He is required to be constantly at hand, and must even lurk patiently outside the fitting room when Diana is buying dresses.

When the princess is on open view he stands close to her, looking like one of the royal group. But beneath his well-tailored suit, and readily accessible, is his

Above: *An evening at the Royal Opera House*
Left: *In Hyde Park to plant a cherry tree*

firearm. The cost of guarding royalty is a high one. Additional security at Highgrove added £50,000 a year to the local police budget, a sum that the ratepayers are obliged to meet. According to Godfrey Smith, columnist on *The Sunday Times* and a nearby resident, they pay up with a smile, aware that the royal presence has put several thousand pounds on the value of their properties. A tumbledown cottage of no architectural interest was sold at auction for a sum more in keeping with a mews house in Kensington, simply because its rear windows had a clear view directly over the Highgrove estate. But anyone who attempted to enter the grounds, or worse still, to break into the house, would come up against a fearsome electronic alarm system that would rouse the entire Tetbury police force, to say nothing of the security men on the premises. A small cottage in the grounds has been turned into a police station.

Highgrove is a surprisingly modest house in comparison with other royal homes, and set alongside Althorp it would scarcely show at all. It was built in 1798 for John Paul Paul, a Huguenot whose immigrant family had settled in the Cotswolds and prospered from clothmaking. The name of the architect is not known. The most impressive part of the house is the 40-foot entrance hall and its broad staircase, with the main reception rooms one each side. Upstairs are four bedrooms and the nursery on the first floor, a further nine bedrooms on the second floor. There are stables and a surrounding wooded estate of 350 acres. It was an imaginative gesture of the locals to give as their wedding present a handsome set of wrought-iron gates for the main entrance.

Dudley Poplak has transformed the interior. His alterations cost an additional £250,000 on top of the £800,000 that Charles had paid for the property.

The actual number of staff required to run the house has been limited to a butler and three footmen, three maids and a cook-housekeeper. Already there has been a turnover among the household staff. Charles lost his valet, who complained of arguments between the Princess and himself over the Prince's clothes. Another blow was the departure of the recently-appointed cook to get married. The jobs of royal servants, in spite of their obvious social cachet, are rarely sinecures, and the financial rewards are minimal, as wages are one of the most closely-watched items on the household budget.

Surprisingly, none of the Princess's ladies-in-waiting are of her generation. Anne Beckwith-Smith, the only one who is full-time, used to work at Sotheby's. The others are Lavinia Baring and Hazel West, both married women. Mrs West is the wife of the assistant comptroller in the Lord Chamberlain's office, the department responsible for stage managing events such as the royal wedding. All three ladies are in their 30s, and are new to the job. It entails accompanying the Princess on any official function she undertakes, smoothing the way over any difficulties and generally providing companionship and support. They liaise with the organisers and are in effect the link between the Princess and the general public. If you write to her, unless you are a personal friend, you will get a letter back signed by one of the ladies-in-waiting, who have to undertake formidable secretarial duties as well. They work on a rota business, are not paid anything more than a token fee, are expected to be well-bred, well-connected, discreet, pleasant, tactful and conservatively-dressed. The rewards are meeting a wide variety of people, becoming a close and valued friend of the Princess and enjoying considerable social prestige.

Christmas 1981 was an active time for the Princess. She and Charles went to a special performance of the ballet *Romeo and Juliet* at the Royal Opera House in celebration of their marriage. Later they went informally to *Tosca* and *Il Trovatore* simply because they enjoy opera. The Friends of Covent Garden gained an important new champion in Diana.

Even the arts in tiny Tetbury did not go unnoticed. A concert in St Mary's Church in aid of the Benjamin Britten Foundation for young musicians was

Right: *Opening Northampton's new Post Office – handy for Althorp*

Children at Guildford Cathedral stage a Nativity play as part of a special concert of Christmas carols

attended by the residents of Highgrove. But Diana's most significant local engagement was a visit to St Mary's Church of England Junior School in Tetbury. The snow was ankle deep, the sky blue, the air crisp and cold. The Princess turned up at the wheel of her own car, sat with the children for their morning assembly, sang carols with them, toured the school and stayed for more than two hours among the overjoyed youngsters who had hardly dared hope that she would accept their invitation made when her engagement to Prince Charles was announced. Her easy, relaxed way with children was totally evident that day.

There were a few more carol services on a more elaborate scale to be attended before the Christmas holiday itself. There was Gloucester, celebrating the cathedral's 1300th anniversary. There was Guildford, where the children took part in a nativity play. Outside the snow whirled down, but the waiting crowds were rewarded with a sight of the Princess defying the seasonal weather.

Then came her first royal Christmas at Windsor. The Queen gathers the family under the commodious roof of the largest inhabited castle in the world each year for an old-fashioned celebration. The Queen Mother, the Kents, the Gloucesters, Princess Alexandra and her family, Princess Anne and hers, Princess Margaret and all the royal children foregather for a house party approaching in size, but not in solemnity, those of Queen Victoria's day. At Windsor yuletides in George VI's reign his daughters performed in their own pantomimes. For Christmas 1981 Charles invited the Bach Choir to the Castle to entertain the assembly.

The public part of Christmas celebration is the morning service on December 25 at St George's Chapel. Afterwards in the pale December sunshine the small, distinguished congregation stood on the steps chatting among themselves while the photographers busily snapped away. The Princess was snugly wrapped in a coat that was the same shade of royal blue as

that of the Queen.

After Christmas the party split up. The Queen, Prince Philip, Andrew and Edward were joined at Sandringham by Charles, Diana and the Queen Mother. Diana regards herself as a Norfolk person, having been born and raised on the Sandringham estate, and a return to the county is like a homecoming for her. Park House has remained unoccupied since her father inherited the Spencer title, but during the New Year holiday she went over to have a look round the place and think back to her childhood. The previous Christmas and New Year had been spent at Althorp, well away from Charles and Sandringham, then ringed with photographers expecting Lady Diana Spencer to break cover. Now she was in the setting she had so determinedly set out to reach. It is possible that she wished she could have invited a few of her old friends along, for her husband's family makes a formidable crowd *en masse*, and would still be eagerly sizing her up. It helped that Prince Andrew was a childhood friend.

Above: *School Fair at Tulse Hill, Brixton, January 1982*
Left: *Outside St George's Chapel, Windsor, Christmas morning*
Below: *It seems that the camera still takes getting used to*

Ahead lay a difficult year. The memories of the royal wedding of 1981 were relived on television at the end of the year, and then passed into the national folklore. The Princess was now three months pregnant and preparing for the summer event. Already she was wearing maternity outfits, and had scooped up much of the stock at Jasper Conran's trendy emporium. Soon she was to start having them made-to-measure. She also went on a course of Royal Jelly capsules, an expensive way to keep up the vitality during pregnancy, probably greatly approved by Countess Spencer's mother, Barbara Cartland, whose regard for magical potions has enabled her to reach advanced years with scarcely an outward sign.

A contretemps followed a short break the couple took in the Bahamas in February. They were staying in a small resort on Eleuthra, in what was thought to be a secluded setting. Unfortunately the *paparazzi* were for once smarter than the Prince, and from a nearby beach a photographer was able to secure a reasonably-sharp picture of a bikini-clad

Above: *Sir Geoffrey Howe greets guests for dinner at No. 11 to discuss film preservation*
Left: *The Princess goes to the Barbican*

Right: *Another night of music at the Royal Albert Hall, Kensington*
Inset: *Little Foxes premiere and Elizabeth Taylor*

Diana with a slightly-bulging midriff. Newspapers all over the world published it, including two in Fleet Street, the *Daily Star* and *The Sun*. There followed a righteous uproar, to some extent fanned by other tabloids that had been unable to buy the picture themselves. The Queen, it was said, was frothing with indignation over it. A silly public debate took place on whether or not photographs of a pregnant woman were offensive, uncovering a host of lurking Freudian taboos. The prevailing view was that some barrier of good taste had been broached, and the newspapers concerned were urged to make a suitable apology. The response of *The Sun* was a vigorous defence of its policy, and an apology so patently insincere that it was accompanied by a repetition of the so-called offensive picture. It was hard not to see their point. Diana, pregnant or not, was a charming sight in a bikini.

Unsurprisingly, once again Fleet Street found itself in bad odour. The rota system of reporting, the dreaded bane of every news editor, was invoked to minimise the pressure on the Princess. But the fact was that Diana, a singularly photogenic female, attracted cameras wherever she went. If it wasn't the

motor-driven Nikons of the professionals it was the Instamatics of the man and woman in the street. It was a hazard of life with which it was necessary for her to come to terms or succumb from severe psychological trauma. The orchestra of clicking shutters and spitting strobes will be a familiar accompaniment to all her performances for many years to come.

One of the effects of marriage common not only to royals is to turn previously gregarious, outgoing people, each with a large circle of friends, into homebodies. Although the Prince and Diana were both active socially there was little overlap. It is hardly surprising in view of the fact that he is 13 years her senior, and has led a remarkably full life already, having travelled the world, served in both the Royal Air Force and the Royal Navy, and held commands. He is also a university man, and his Archaeology and Anthropology degree acquired when he was at Trinity College, Cambridge was a respectable 2:1. Diana on the other hand left school at 16 without so much as an O level, was engaged at 19 and married when she was barely 20.

There is bound, consequently, to be a substantial generation gap. Diana annoyed her stepmother by playing loud

Door 8

Left: *Teatime in Huddersfield – a rapt Princess*
Above: *Practising the art of conversation*

Abba and Dire Straits records through the Althorp hi-fi. Now she keeps it to herself with a Sony Walkman clamped to her head. It sometimes means that she is unaware of what is going on around her, and even the Queen has sometimes found herself ignored by an oblivious Diana, enclosed in her own world of enveloping sound that only she can hear.

She likes to read a lot, but mostly paperbacks which are bought by the armful and include a large number of romantic stories. Whether or not she stays abreast of the works of Barbara Cartland, a one-woman industry of novelettes, with a backlist running into several hundreds, is not known.

As has been seen, she also eats a lot of sweets, although, in spite of that, her teeth are in good shape. During pregnancy the sweet-tooth cravings had probably been accentuated. She even drops discarded sweet papers on expensive carpets like a wayward child. It has to be remembered that for Diana there has always been someone to pick them up, but the harmless little habit caused some eyebrows to ascend at Buckingham Palace. Not, it should be said, those of Prince Charles, who accepted the trivial peccadilloes of his loved one with a manly, if not besotted, generosity.

There are a number of shared tastes. Music is one of them, although her enthusiasms range much more broadly across the spectrum than his, which have been refined by many years of maturity. They are both fond of opera and ballet. The Princess is a skilful dancer, and can tap dance with style, possibly encouraging Charles to loosen his feet in a similar manner. They have large music rooms both at Highgrove and Kensington Palace, and like to fill their houses with sound from the extensive collection of records and tapes.

Both are good skiers, and the cancellation of the winter trip to Switzerland was one of the most hard-to-bear sacrifices of pregnancy. Her interest in polo has been developed since her relationship with Charles began, but not without controversy. Some of the Prince's old friends feel that she has interfered with this particular enthusiasm and tried to stop him from playing. Newspaper photographs have occasionally caught her pouting and looking bored at matches. It was while the Prince was playing that she had her most-

Delighting the crowds in Liverpool. The Princess and a child who will now have something to remember always

prominent bout of tears in front of the cameras.

The Prince is a skilled, vigorous and aggressive player, as is his father, and bears scars to show it. His injuries have given the Queen cause for alarm, so it is highly likely that his wife would also seek to discourage such an active participation in the sport that it would put his limbs at risk. Charles did indeed modify his interest, and has reduced the number of times he takes to the field. It is quite possible that he made the decision unprompted as the sobering responsibilities of husband and future father assailed his conscience. Diana has subsequently denied the canard that she hates polo, claiming that the opposite is true and that she really enjoys it.

They both enjoy each other's company to the exclusion of their former circles. Friends of both the Prince and Diana have said that they have scarcely set eyes on them since the marriage. Where both would have been out dining they are now content to stay at home watching television and munching an informal meal from a tray. It is scarcely surprising that given the hectic conditions prevailing in almost any public engagement they crave their moments of privacy when they can retreat from the clamour and just be with each other. During a weekend at Althorp the Princess prevailed upon her disappointed step-

During the arduous months surrounding the Coronation he scarcely saw his mother. Diana had the misfortune to suffer from a broken home when she was hardly any older. The departure of her mother had a disturbing effect on her upbringing, and brought a sadness to her childhood for which there never can be any real compensation. Her mother was, and is very much part of her life, and they share certain similarities of outlook, particularly in their strong-willed determination to be individuals. But the custody battle made its indelible impression.

Therefore Diana will insist on being as close as possible to her children, and the Prince will support her. The nanny she has engaged is not a starchy Norland-trained type, but one with an informal, modern manner with whom she will have a close rapport. Diana knows from her own experience that child psy-

Above left: Vantage point for the Grand National
Below left: Aintree anxiety – "Will we win?"
Above: The new Sony plant gets advertised
Right: Arriving to open Sony factory, Bridgend

mother not to have any parties or invited guests for all the time that they were there.

They both love the country, but are likely to move from Highgrove in a few years to a better house. Diana had no say in its selection as the Prince had already bought it before they were engaged, and would like to find a place that she could plan from the outset. Highgrove will suffice for a time, and will eventually be sold at a handsome profit on account of its associations. The new home is most likely to be in the same area. Already there is a Cotswolds royal enclave, with Princess Anne and Mark Phillips at Gatcombe Park and Prince and Princess Michael of Kent at Nether Lypiatt. It is an easily-accessible part of the country, being close to the fast M4 which as well as bringing London within easy reach also serves Windsor Castle and Heathrow.

Both Diana and Charles were left on their own a lot during childhood. Charles had to accept the fact that his mother was often so busily involved in affairs of state that he had to be pushed to the background. The Queen came to the throne when he was only three years old.

chologists are right in stressing the importance for both child and mother in having close contact during the early years. The old-fashioned practice of banishing the children unseen to the nursery and the iron control of a nanny is not going to occur in her home, and it is likely that the Prince himself will quickly master the mysterious knack of correctly folding a nappy. Babies, once a source of embarrassment for the bachelor Prince as he moved among the people, are now a topic of interest for him, and he has been seen to grin happily at those he encounters. In some ways Diana's effect on him has been more drastic than his on her. It has even been said that she, having inherited her mother's tenacity and sense of purpose, is the one wearing the trousers, and the Prince, used to a lifetime of bossing others, is bemusedly happy to have his domestic life so ably looked after. He is alleged to have become more relaxed and patient.

It is still hard for Diana's old friends to have to call her 'Your Royal Highness' and 'ma'am', at least in the presence of others, and her husband 'sir'. Some members of the royal family become steely-eyed if such courtesies are not observed, and there is a special glare

reserved for those who have overstepped the mark. Princess Margaret has even been known to sweep from the dinner table after an unduly familiar remark. Diana is unlikely to react in such a manner, but already she has cultivated a style of reproval that leaves the person on the receiving end in no doubt. It comes in the form of a long look with the head tilted sideways, a sort of 'I don't believe it!' expression on her face. It is not widely-appreciated that there are only two women in the land who do not have to drop curtseys to her on official occasions, the Queen and the Queen Mother. To them it is Diana who must make the ancient genuflection, and in royal circles it is customary for the Queen to receive a curtsey even in a totally informal setting, although she has gone a long way towards abolishing the previously-rigid adherence to the old forms of bowing and scraping.

Diana is officially Her Royal Highness the Princess of Wales, and not Princess Diana, because she married the bearer of the princely title, and was not made a princess in her own right. Some pedantic adherents to royal form would have liked her to be known as the Princess Charles, but clearly such an unfeminine desig-

The Princess, radiantly pregnant, visits the Scilly Isles, as the Duke of Cornwall looks at the Duchy

Above: Babies now evoke a special interest for the royal couple
Right: Gingerly negotiating Scillies steps

nation was not going to be acceptable to the public. Others argued that 'Princess Diana' was not a solecism because before her marriage, as the daughter of an earl, she was styled Lady Diana Spencer, and the term 'Lady' was synonymous with 'Princess'. To millions she *is* 'Princess Diana' or popularly 'Princess Di', but privately she dislikes the diminutive form of her name. Diana is not a name that has been found in the House of Windsor before, and while it is common enough (and one of those classless names that can be found in any demographic group in Britain) it is said to lack a royal ring. It is wondered whether or not she will become Queen Diana or adopt another name. It is possible that Charles will not become Charles III but use one of his other names – Philip, Arthur or George. The Christian names used by the royal family are generally very conventional, although Princess Anne's daughter has been called Zara.

While the Queen has never participated in a direct face-to-face television interview, royal broadcasting has become much more relaxed during her reign. Both the Duke of Edinburgh and Prince Charles have been interviewed on special occasions or on behalf of particular causes and have acquitted themselves in a professional manner. The closest the Queen has got to an easy camera style was during the making of Richard Cawston's joint BBC/ITV documentary *The Royal Family* in 1969. Diana and Charles have faced both television interviewers and newspaper reporters without qualms, although careful stage managing has ensured that they were not faced with unexpected questions. Nevertheless, it is something that the Queen has never submitted herself to, and her distaste and nervousness of such situations showed during President Reagan's famous Windsor ride when American TV news reporters attempted to question him in the Queen's embarrassed presence.

Charles and Diana may have a very long time to go before they are king and queen. Whatever talk there is of the Queen abdicating at retirement age, such a possibility is unlikely. Her sense of duty and faith is such that to her the throne is not some pensionable post to be vacated and passed to the next in line when the joints stiffen but a sacred trust and God-given mission to the people. Whatever the popular view of the monarchy as a special kind of spectacular pageant, a branch of show business, the Queen guards its spiritual meaning, ever conscious of the vow of service she made in 1947 on her 21st birthday. Prince Charles, always ready, should not expect to accede until the next century. By then the youthfulness of Diana will have a positive advantage as she will only be in her thirties as the 21st century begins.

Meanwhile, the Charles and Diana years have already begun and the British people have just cause for celebration. For his Diana is our Diana, and there is the promise of much excitement in the years ahead.

Overleaf: *Three faces of impending motherhood, at Duxford, Cambs.*

The polo-playing prince, said to be easing-up on his sport

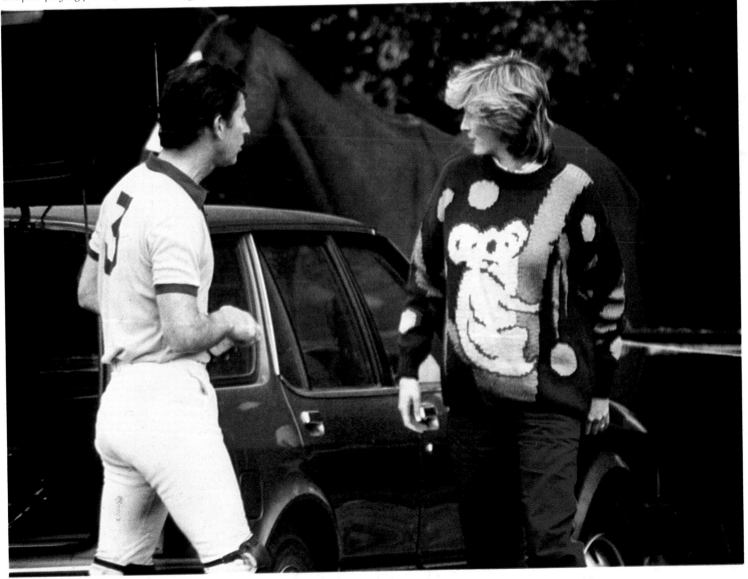

The Royal Horoscope

by Julia Parker

The Royal Baby, born with Sagittarius rising, the sun and moon in Cancer, and under the midheaven of Scorpio.

The Sun had entered Cancer a little over an hour before the young Prince's birth, and because he was born at the time of the new Moon, Cancer is also his Moon-sign. So the general characteristics attributed to Cancer – tenderness, tenacity, an instinctive protectiveness and a high emotional capacity with strong intuition and sensitivity – will not only be decidedly marked in his personality but in his immediate reactions to all situations. It might be thought that because he was born 'on the cusp', he will have some Geminian characteristics; but as far as the Sun's position is concerned, this is not the case. However, his thinking processes will most certainly be spiced with lively Geminian facets, as at the time of his birth Mercury was in Gemini, making him talkative, very quick-witted, and with a natural ability to put his ideas over in an easy-flowing and amusing, witty way.

The all-important rising-sign, Sagittarius, is an interesting counter to his Cancerian qualities, and in many ways we will over the years see some well above-average striking resemblances to his mother (the Princess of Wales has both a Cancerian Sun and a Sagittarian Ascendant). Because of the influence of his rising sign, and other elements in his birth chart, the Prince will have a tremendous breadth of vision, and he will enjoy challenge. He'll be versatile and brave, and will, like his father, have too little time in which to get through everything he'll want to do. On the negative side, he'll have to be carefully trained to overcome considerable restlessness, and changes of mood could be something of a problem. He has lashings of imagination – and this too will need quite a lot of careful direction, since he could be more than a little carried away by it at times, and when he is a child could for instance tend to make up highly imaginative stories which turn out not, actually, to be entirely true!

As there is a genetic pattern working through parents and children, so there is a decided astrological one when the charts of two or more generations are compared. The Prince of Wales sun-sign is Scorpio, which was the sign on the Midheaven at the time of his son's birth – a typical link between father and son, and one which denotes an excellent sense of identification with each others objectives. They may not always agree, but each will certainly understand what the other is getting at or seeking to achieve.

The chart overall is an excellent one in many ways, and perhaps the most fascinating feature is the fact that due to the fact that the Sagittarian Ascendant, Jupiter, which rules the young Prince's chart, was culminating – i.e., right at the top of the sky – when he was born. An important placing indeed, and one which, after a very great deal of research involving thousands of charts, emerges strongly in the birth-charts of actors and actresses. So he will carry out the role of Prince and eventually King with flair, panache and a breath-taking sense of drama!

Saturn was also high in the sky, among other planets, and because of this the theme of responsibility emerges very strongly. So does a psychological need for total involvement in his work, energy, and a need for job satisfaction. Whatever station of life he had been born into, no ordinary, dull, routine job would have suited him. However, in no way will his life be all work and no play, for a splendidly placed Venus in Taurus (yet another placing he shares with the Princess) should ensure that he enjoys life – good food and beautiful things – and that he has an affectionate and loving nature. This placing can also contribute a considerable appreciation of the arts, and potential for artistic talent.

The chart is in many ways an excellent one, and provided the Prince's tendency to restlessness is gently but firmly controlled and his imagination directed positively, Prince Charles and Princess Diana should thoroughly enjoy bringing up their son.

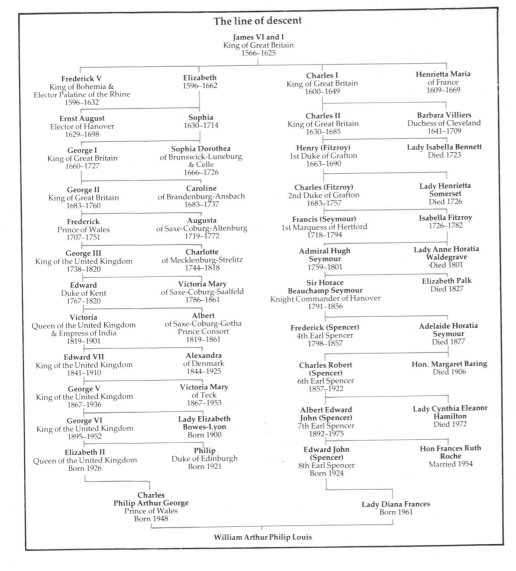

The line of descent

James VI and I
King of Great Britain
1566–1625

Frederick V King of Bohemia & Elector Palatine of the Rhine 1596–1632	Elizabeth 1596–1662	Charles I King of Great Britain 1600–1649	Henrietta Maria of France 1609–1669
Ernst August Elector of Hanover 1629–1698	Sophia 1630–1714	Charles II King of Great Britain 1630–1685	Barbara Villiers Duchess of Cleveland 1641–1709
George I King of Great Britain 1660–1727	Sophia Dorothea of Brunswick-Luneburg & Celle 1666–1726	Henry (Fitzroy) 1st Duke of Grafton 1663–1690	Lady Isabella Bennett Died 1723
George II King of Great Britain 1683–1760	Caroline of Brandenburg-Ansbach 1683–1737	Charles (Fitzroy) 2nd Duke of Grafton 1683–1757	Lady Henrietta Somerset Died 1726
Frederick Prince of Wales 1707–1751	Augusta of Saxe-Coburg-Altenburg 1719–1772	Francis (Seymour) 1st Marquess of Hertford 1718–1794	Isabella Fitzroy 1726–1782
George III King of the United Kingdom 1738–1820	Charlotte of Mecklenburg-Strelitz 1744–1818	Admiral Hugh Seymour 1759–1801	Lady Anne Horatia Waldegrave Died 1801
Edward Duke of Kent 1767–1820	Victoria Mary of Saxe-Coburg-Saalfeld 1786–1861	Sir Horace Beauchamp Seymour Knight Commander of Hanover 1791–1856	Elizabeth Palk Died 1827
Victoria Queen of the United Kingdom & Empress of India 1819–1901	Albert of Saxe-Coburg-Gotha Prince Consort 1819–1861	Frederick (Spencer) 4th Earl Spencer 1798–1857	Adelaide Horatia Seymour Died 1877
Edward VII King of the United Kingdom 1841–1910	Alexandra of Denmark 1844–1925	Charles Robert (Spencer) 6th Earl Spencer 1857–1922	Hon. Margaret Baring Died 1906
George V King of the United Kingdom 1867–1936	Victoria Mary of Teck 1867–1953	Albert Edward John (Spencer) 7th Earl Spencer 1892–1975	Lady Cynthia Eleanor Hamilton Died 1972
George VI King of the United Kingdom 1895–1952	Lady Elizabeth Bowes-Lyon Born 1900	Edward John (Spencer) 8th Earl Spencer Born 1924	Hon Frances Ruth Roche Married 1954
Elizabeth II Queen of the United Kingdom Born 1926	Philip Duke of Edinburgh Born 1921		

Charles
Philip Arthur George
Prince of Wales
Born 1948

Lady Diana Frances
Born 1961

William Arthur Philip Louis

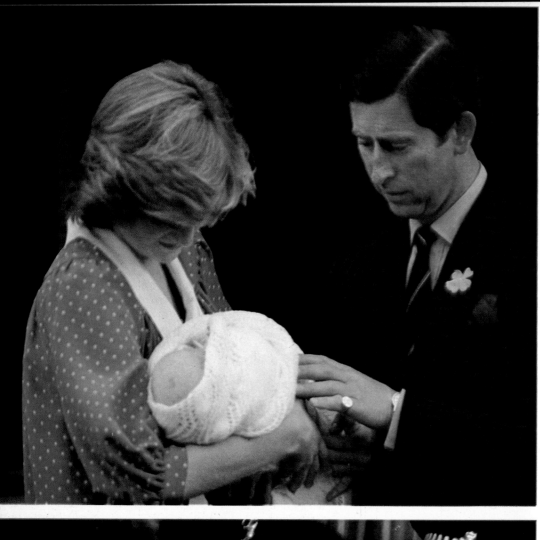

It was the longest day of the year. Shortly after six a.m. on June 21 Diana went into the Lindo Wing of St Mary's Hospital, Paddington, where Mr George Pinker's delivery room is located. Prince Charles went in with her and remained for the long hours before the birth. Outside crowds gathered.

At three minutes past nine that evening, still daylight in London, a boy was born.

"It's a Prince!" said Alastair Burnet, introducing ITN's News at Ten a short while later. A happy nation went to bed.

The following day the Queen, Earl Spencer and Mrs Shand Kydd with Lady Jane Fellowes came to see the new baby, second-in-line to the throne. Prince Charles happily chatted to reporters and the crowd. "What about another?" asked one. "Give us a chance!" he said. Then, to everyone's surprise, at the end of the afternoon, the royal couple, Diana looking relaxed and blooming, appeared on the hospital steps with their son. Such was the excellent physical shape of the young mother that she could take her child home less than a day after delivery. With smiles, waves and great happiness, they drove off to Kensington Palace and home.

The Prince's eyes were firmly shut, but the crowds were able to glimpse the tip of William's tiny head – enough to furnish a sighting of the next monarch but one.

Her stay in hospital was relatively short, but Mr Pinker, aware of her good health and sound physique, readily agreed to permit her to leave less than 24 hours after the birth. There is always the risk of hospital infection, and a mother is usually happier in her home surroundings. In any case, everything had been made ready at Kensington Palace. And above all, the crowds waiting outside the hospital were treated to their view of the young prince far sooner than they had expected.

In Parliament both Mrs Thatcher, the Prime Minister, and Mr Michael Foot, the Leader of the Opposition, concurred in expressing the congratulations of the House. Telegrams and messages poured in from all round the world – on the one hand the formal expressions of goodwill from heads of state in friendly countries, on the other simple letters of joy from children, old age pensioners and ordinary people, touched by the birth of the most important royal baby since 1948, when the Prince of Wales was born.

After a few days at Kensington the young prince, nestling in his mother's arms, set out on the journey by car to Highgrove, a police escort discreetly smoothing a way for the Ford Granada with its royal cargo on the rear seat.

The names chosen for the prince were regarded as satisfactory both by progressives and traditionalists. William Arthur Philip Louis. The last monarch to be called William was William IV, who died in 1837, while Arthur is a name not borne by a British king since the mystical days of the Round Table. Philip, one of Prince Charles' own names, is derived from the baby prince's paternal grandfather, and Louis is in honour of Lord Mountbatten, whose influence on the Prince of Wales was close and powerful.

A happy decision was made to stage the Christening on the same day that the Queen Mother attained the age of 82 – August 4. But meanwhile, the Princess was to make a public appearance, attending the special memorial service at St. Paul's Cathedral on July 26, for those who died in the short war in the Falklands between Britain and the invading Argentinians. It was not an occasion without controversy, as some would have preferred it to have been an overt "victory" service, but the Church of England and its senior prelate, the Archbishop of Canterbury, were at pains

Anniversary portraits by Lord Snowdon.
Prince William was a month old

to keep any form of jingoism out of the Cathedral, and instead to offer prayers for those who died on both sides. All of the Queen's immediate family attended the service with the exceptions of Prince Edward, and Prince Andrew, who was still on active duty in the South Atlantic as a naval helicopter pilot. He had acquitted himself particularly well in dangerous situations, and had earned considerable popularity for performing his assignment without any special consideration, taking the rough with the smooth alongside his less-exalted shipmates. Charles, during a public engagement in Croydon, revealed that his brother had written in a letter to Diana that "he had never been so frightened in his life."

Left: *Leaving St Paul's after the Falklands service – Princess Anne behind*
Below: *Queen Mother, Prince Charles and Princess at the Falklands service*

The Christening took place in the Music Room of Buckingham Palace, and was conducted by Dr Runcie, the Archbishop. By then the baby prince was all of 44 days old. Many of the royal guests wore blue in his honour, but his mother only had subtle traces of the colour in a predominantly pink floral-patterned dress. Four generations were present, with the Queen Mother proudly holding her great-grandson for the camera. The baby endured the baptism with equanimity, but lost some of his patience during the photographic session, letting go with a powerful pair of tiny lungs. The Queen and the Queen Mother tried to still the sobs without success. Prince Charles then made an attempt with similar ineffectiveness. Only when Diana offered him her little finger did he fall silent, contentedly sucking at it.

As well as Prince Charles and Prince Philip others present included Princess Anne and Captain Mark Phillips,

Princess Alexandra and her husband Angus Ogilvy, Prince Edward, ex-King Constantine of the Hellenes and ex-Queen Marie, Lord Romsey, the Duchess of Westminster, Lady Susan Hussey, Earl Spencer, Mrs Shand Kydd, Ruth Lady Fermoy and Sir Laurens van der Post. Prince William wore the traditional royal christening robe made from Honiton lace and white satin that had done service for some of those present, including his father.

For Diana the summer of 1982 was perforce a quiet one. The excitement of the previous year, with the last days of the engagement, the wedding and the honeymoon, now belonged firmly to the past, as the couple reached their first anniversary, and she made the adjustments to motherhood, as well as celebrating her 21st birthday. The reminders of her brief life as a single girl faded. The flat at Coleherne Court was sold, fetching somewhat less than the

asking price of £100,000 in the strained economic climate. The new owner was obliged to promise not to mention any royal connection should he sell within five years, nor to allow film companies access to the premises.

In August the traditional royal pilgrimage was made to Balmoral. There was some agitation that Charles and Diana had flouted part of that tradition by travelling together to Aberdeen in the same Andover of the Queen's Flight, accompanied by the baby prince in a carrycot. There is a rule that principal members of the royal family do not fly together for safety reasons, and normally Charles and Andrew are never on the same aircraft, nor do they fly with the Queen. For two heirs to be on the same flight, particularly one of the elderly piston-engined Andovers, with Charles spending part of the time at the controls, was enough to cause a jump in the national heartbeat and a nervous edi-

torial in *The Times*, which nevertheless concluded that in his early years it was better that the risk be taken rather than part the little Prince William from his parents.

Diana has consistently made it plain that she intends to spend much time with the child, and any that follow subsequently, particularly during their earliest years. But for William there will always be the most special attention, for he is the second in the line-of-succession, and as he grows older the responsibilities will close in on him; the realisation of the awesome task one day to befall him will emerge in the special tuition in statecraft that he will receive, as did his father. Prince Charles revealed in an interview with an American reporter (questions relating to his marriage and fatherhood were specifically barred) something of the intensely claustrophobic nature of the upbringing of the heir to the throne, and of the difficulties

The Christening party: seated, Princess Anne, the Queen, Princess of Wales and Prince William, the Queen Mother, Mrs Shand Kydd. Behind, Captain Mark Phillips, the Duke of Edinburgh, Angus Ogilvy, ex-Queen Marie, Princess Alexandra, ex-King Constantine, Lady Susan Hussey, the Prince of Wales, Lord Romsey, the Duchess of Westminster, Earl Spencer, Ruth Lady Fermoy, Sir Laurens van der Post, Prince Edward

Right: *Four generations of royalty – the Queen Mother dandles great-grandson*

in pursuing any worthwhile objective without incurring criticism from one side or another. His experience in coping with it will clearly be of enormous benefit to his son, just as the presence of Diana is going to make life easier in many ways for him.

Clear differences in style were visible after a year of marriage. Never re-nowned as a fashion leader, possessing a wardrobe of Savile Row suits of such timeless cut that they are never noticed, Charles has however gained a certain jauntiness. The Princess had even begun to have *her* shirts made by Turnbull and Asser. She has also encouraged her husband to forsake the traditional haircut which did little to divert attention from his prominent ears, and to allow her own hairstylist, Kevin Shanley, to have a go, with interesting results. Charles has given many signs of enjoying the new influence in his life, even if it has meant saying goodbye to many of his bachelor interests and friends. Diana, as has been shown again and again, is not a shrinking violet, never a "Shy Di" – an epithet dreamed up by a tired Fleet Street sub-editor because it made a good headline-fit – but an extraordinarily forthright, determined young woman, with a very clear idea of what she wants. Her gifts are many, not least her ability to get on with people, to charm the most hardened and surly, as well as those who would already have been willing to eat out of her hand. She has an uncanny

Left: *Prince Charles with parents and grandmother, wife and son*

Below: *A maternal little finger soothes the infant prince at Christening*

instinct, more common to Hollywood superstars, of knowing just what cameras are going to do to her, and of nearly always being ready for the click of the shutter. Photographers doing the Diana-round have often been amazed at the number of good shots they have been able to get of her. Most people are invariably caught looking down or away or grumpy or asleep, even if they are royalty. The bad pictures of Diana, however, are rare, and sometimes the unguarded moments produce results as good as those that are the fruits of a long sitting. She has a quick mind, and can make lightening responses to questions, which while not exactly having the polish of Wildean epigrams, show her to have wit as well as good humour. Above all, she has an unstuffy way with her, and although her upbringing, for all the trauma of her parents' divorce, was sheltered and privileged in stately homes and vast country estates, she is perfectly at ease talking to the humble, the poor, the old, the handicapped, without a trace of any patronising, bogus, upper-class manner. Children immediately recognise her genuine naturalness and achieve an instant rapport.

She is, without doubt, a new national asset, a presence that gives the British people pleasure, pride and satisfaction. That their future king could have been so fortunate in his choice of wife, of finding a girl whose Britishness exceeded his own as a glance at her family tree reveals, and who radiates so many special qualities as well as striking beauty, must count as the great achievement of his life thus far.

© Windward 1982

Published in this edition by
Windward, an imprint of
W H Smith & Son Ltd.
Registered No. 237811, England.

Trading as
WHS Publishers Inc., 112 Madison Avenue,
New York, NY 10016

ISBN 0 8317 2206 1

Written by George Perry
Picture research by Vincent Page

Designed by Tim McPhee
Design & production in association with
Book Production Consultants, Cambridge

Set by Goodfellow & Egan Phototypesetting Ltd,
Cambridge
Printed in England by Sir Joseph Causton and Sons Ltd,
and bound by R J Acford, Chichester.

Photographic acknowledgements:

Anwar Hussein: 1, 17, 18/19 top centre, 24, 26
bottom, 28, 38 top left, 48 bottom, 53, 54 top,
55 bottom, 56, 57 bottom, 58 right, 62, 63, 72
Camera Press: 6, 8 top right & top left, 64, 65
Central Press: 8 bottom, 10, 11 right, 23 inset left,
40 bottom, 47 bottom right & top right, 48 right,
50, 54 bottom
Colour Library International: 38 bottom left
Fox Photos: 42 top, 46, 49, 51, 55 top
Ken Goff/Frank Spooner: 21
Gamma/Frank Spooner: 23 inset right, 33 top left
Photographers International: Front endpaper,
3 bottom, 4, 22 inset, 25, 27 top left & bottom right,
34/35, 44 left, 47 left, 58 top left, 60 full & bottom
inset, 66 top left, 71, Back end paper
Press Association: 2, 3 top 70
Rex Features: 5, 12, 18 bottom, 20, 27 top right, 31,
44 right, 52, 57 top, 59, 60 top left inset, Back cover
Syndication International: 9 right, 14, 15, 19, 29, 32,
33 top right, 36, 37, 40 top, 41 right, 43, 45, 66, 67, 68/6
71 bottom right
Tim Graham: Front cover 7, 9 left, 11 left, 13, 16,
22/23, 26 top, 30, 33 bottom, 38/39, 41 left, 42 bottom